Nothing Will Be As Sweet As the Taste

Selected poems 1974 — 1994

Elana Dykewomon

Published in 1995 by Onlywomen Press Limited
Radical Feminist Lesbian Publishers
40 St. Lawrence Terrace, London W10 5ST

ISBN 0 906500 57 5

The following poems were previously published: "A Law of Physics," *Bridges*, Vol. 4, No.
1, 1994, Eugene, OR; "The Census Taker Interviews the 20th Century" *Bridges*, Vol. 3,
No. 1, 1992; "Oakland: February 1991, 1AM," *Sinister Wisdom* #46, Berkeley, CA, 1992;
"the real fat womon poems," *Sinister Wisdom* #43/44, 1991; "Knowledge in the Biblical
Sense" and "Carnal Knowledge" in Sinister Wisdom #31, 1987; "Even My Eyes Become
Mouths," *Naming the Waves — Contemporary Lesbian Poetry,* Virago Press, London, 1988
Crossing Press, Freedom, CA,1990; "If you were my home..." and "Fifteen Miles from the
KKK," *Poetry Readings of the IV International Feminist Bookfair*, Barcelona, Spain, 1990;
"Fifteen Miles from the KKK," *Nice Jewish Girls — A Lesbian Anthology,* Beacon Press,
Boston,1989. The poems "If you were my home" and "15 Miles from the KKK" were
included on the tape "Dyke Proud," from the poetry reading at the 1988 3rd
International Feminist Bookfair in Montreal, Annor Productions, Montreal, Canada, 1988.

Printed and bound in Great Britain by Redwood Books, Trowbridge, Wiltshire.

British Library/Cataloguing-in-Publication Data. A catalogue record for this book
is available from the British Library.

For all the lesbians who've trusted me with their intimate words
especially my first lover & lasting friend, Eva
my kin-spirits Dolphin and Susan Jill
my partner & lover Susan

Contents

ॐ If you were my home
I would be your garden

If I was your garden   I would want you
to cultivate me to plant water weed harvest
and like I promised   I would feed you

You can always eat what straggles up or
what's gone to seed but   nothing will be
as sweet   as the taste of the womon
you tended purposefully

she says she is

she says she is air   she says she is fire   she says she is water she
says she is earth
                    then they laugh at her   they say:
                                            you are not all these things
let's see your chart
produce your papers   sweetheart
and your past

                    but my past did not imagine me here
                        on the edge of cliffs
                                    at the boundary of air
                            making fire out of water
                        knocking on the hearts of metal and wood

            and flesh of course flesh
                                    which is the lesbian   element

they forget to mention

A lesbian's prerogative

It's a lesbian's prerogative to run her hand down the seam
        across the seam of need
        and stick her finger in
        where the stitch is loose

a lesbian prerogative
        to pull at the thread, rip it apart
        demand the womyn
        start over

a lesbian prerogative to name herself:
        I am here before
        naming begins before
        phyla and genera   I am
    the species who laughs
        looking at herself in the water
        who crows across the
        the river basin: beware
            my name is hot pepper and sea salt
            my name is spice
            I must be used
            with knowledge of effect
        I change the chemistry
            of the day I enter
            I am the hidden reactor
            I have a half-life of millennia

I can be forced   turned to stone
        underground   I can be hidden
        in storehouses   untapped
        my name can be erased from
        the pillars and tombs
                 still I come back

I am the lesbian lesbians are afraid of —
        the one who says
        you can't have it easy

it doesn't work both ways there's
no polite company   no
diligence with which
you can coin a phrase
that will change the root
        of men's culture
                        and make it safe

it's a lesbian prerogative
        to prophecy
        to rant and demand
        a clear enemy defined
        when she becomes a moving target
        to expect her friends
        to track the source
        of what harms us

it's a lesbian's prerogative
        never to apologize
        to rip at the seams until
        she's satisfied
        and, once satisfied,
                        to doubt satisfaction
                        and start again.

Knowledge in the Biblical Sense

To know her as if in pages. Not any pages. The great pages.
To know her among the great pages, where everything is important,
everything matters. Will matter, for centuries.
                             So that, if I say, behold
thy skin shines as foam on the scales of an asp
                                  hundreds of scholars
will debate my meaning, the gesture, the state of mind, the ancient fortress
so long abandoned — and the garden, what herbs grew there?

To know her in the biblical sense,
    verse and line of her creases under the sensitive skin of my thumb,
    the page beginning to soften with age, the paper
    sending up a humming vibration, so that, looking up
    towards the light in the library window, I am overcome with sensation
    that starts one hundredth of a cubit above my knees,
    and an angel speaks out of the light   lo, you are full of passion,
    your dwelling is touched by desire, you must
        make a covenant, a promise, a sacrifice

      in order to so change the meaning of scripture,
                                        you
must know   what route lust goes as it travels to love and how
it touches the imagination of your people
                          to beget
                          your people
                          one by one

        by knowing her in pages
        and making known what is known

throwing the book open
    to our own interpretation   yes, I am pleased
                                     I knew her that way

on land, in the mythical city
           where her hands shaped monuments of clay
           around which naked girls sang
           after the battle, in the midst of harvests
                                   ripe and full
           handing me the page

               I am satisfied
               I knew her
                       that way

Carnal Knowledge

First we had the sacred, and then the profane. Biblical, then carnal.
Sacred, then profane. What's the difference? she mumbled into my neck,
right after her tongue slid out of my ear.

I'll tell you, honey. I wanted to say, but
my mouth was full of her lips, and I was shaking with five pleasures at once.

I could see it though. I mean everyone
knows about me by now, how I stroke my chin in the middle of Trivial
Pursuit, discussing the answer, and they laugh, saying, well, nu, rebbi?

So, nu, the sacred is easier to describe than the profane: The sacred
comes across the plains of time smelling of sandalwood, beating a
tambourine, and her dark hair falls as water over sense — opening the
passages to revelation, bridging the sensate world with the world of prayer,
so that every touch is an act of devotion, of affirmation, of celebration in the
spirit of the universe, the power that moves mountains and shakes seas is
gratified by our union,   and after our union, our reflection upon it —   the way
what is sacred takes hold of us and gives depth and connection to the holy,
the creative unfolding of our days.

Say that again   she said   Mmmmmmmph I said   No, she said,
pushing her hand deep into my thigh,   Say what you want.

I want you   I said
Where she said   In me   I want you in me   I want you hard in me   I said
How hard? she said   Harder I said   I was sweating and shocked,
grabbing at the flesh of her upper arms, wanting more and more of her and
I could see her: how she'd just been, how I had been between her legs and
my whole hand was throbbing in her cunt/ I had been eating her but now
I had one hand moving and twisting, calling to her to open to me   and one
palm pressing against her clit, against the mound, deep into the bone, the
way the brown skin of her thigh creased and winked at me   made my hips
writhe and I ached to fuck her better than I ever had   deeper strong entirely
present in my lust, wanting to make her forget everything but wanting and
she was calling my name, saying fuck me, fuck me   yes   and I was saying it's
so good you're so good I love to fuck you and then she was in me saying:

What's that you said?

Tell me what you want

I was scared to death but
I said it, I was lying there saying fuck me, get inside me, do me good —

13

and
that's carnal knowledge. Just the tip of it too. Even though we say the same
words over and over it's a lot more complicated being profane than being
sacred.

                              I mean
                          getting known
                    isn't something I learned
                       in Sunday School

The Census Taker Interviews the 20th Century

I came to her door in late afternoon.
It was August, she had planted roses
along a path of paving stones, out of date
and affected. The bushes still in bloom
were going past, the smell as ghastly as
roof pitch in that heat.
                              There was a brass knocker
in the shape of a mermaid. Cloying, I remember
I thought, annoyed by mounting evidence
of sentimental materialism. These little things
you can't write in your report
give so much away.
                              She took her time. Some
of my predecessors had praised her
as energetic, bustling; one
found her lists of patents brilliant. A famous
conversationalist in her youth, the last surveyors
found her quarrelsome and trite. Likely

I would be the last. I don't mind. Demographics
are the heart of our times, and I love a shift
in the underpinnings of alliance. I was prepared
for the crone, offering platitudes and
self-serving reminiscences. She demanded
my I.D. before unbolting an assortment of locks.

"Surprised,
aren't you?" A woman in her early twenties
sat before me in a platinum wheelchair. "Come."
She wheeled forty yards down a dark wood-paneled hall,
stained with the stink of onions and garlic. "Can't get
that smell out, believe you me, I've tried everything."

I expected photos, plaques, a velvet portrait
of Castro, Freud or JFK, a bad copy of O'Keefe,
but there was only odor. As we moved,
the odor grew, shifted, changed. Buttery
as a June night by a back-country Idaho lake it

would suddenly burn, ache or gag.
"Like I said, tried everything."

We came to a room
with a glass wall overlooking a concrete patio,
around which cluttered an assortment of
neon and chrome statues. "It was a garden
during the war." When she laughed I could see
her face was thick with make-up. Not hiding
wrinkles, but covering large welts and sores.

"Which war?" she said, mocking me before
I asked. "Let's see, the war to end all wars or
the one for a new world order, or maybe it was
a victory garden, or perhaps I had it paved
after the Boxer rebellion — did we have concrete
then? Of course. You choose, whatever's
convenient."

I was looking for the page
of my forms on diagnosis, trying
to decide between "senile dementia" "post
traumatic stress" and "hysterical conversion"
when she said "Don't bother. I may be sick
but my mind's still strong, and what's

wrong with me isn't listed in your papers."
There's a little box for "complex of
undetermined emotional/physiologic origin"
where I put a check. I had to get on with
the questions. "How many people
live in this house?"
"You children
always ask the obvious. Go ahead, look around,
count," her gesture arched
across flowered wallpaper, old
brown furniture with brass rivets.
There were square spots where
paintings had been removed.
"Look again," she said.

Now I saw ghosts in the chairs,
playing cards on the camelback couch.
Mediterranean women in shirtwaists and
others with rags around their dreads, tall
white men fiddling with watch chains and
men who had clearly died at the bottom
of mines in Ireland, Capetown, Tennessee.

In a flickering circle, as if through a stereopticon,
the shades of women were marching
for the union, the vote, revolution,
peace, civil rights, for control
of their bodies and sexuality.
"If it's a man's world, at least
I organize the parades — but there,
                              look
there —" she gestured at the walls.
What I had taken for flowers were head upon head
of generations. All the races of women
whose eyes demanded to transmit a
particular reality, children both starving and
well-fed, every kind of administrator, clerk,
laborer vied for my diminishing clarity.

"Well, of course I've had a family, but now
I'm happy to live alone," the images broke apart
with her voice, and I noticed with relief
the gleam of her simple, polished piano.
"Occupation?"
                    "Let's say I — sing, yes,
quite well. Do you know the Marseillais? My
grandmother taught it to me, it's one of my
favorites but I can do Billie Holiday or
rock opera as easily. Would you
care for me to sing to you?"
                              This time I was
quick. "No. No, what's your source of income?"
"Income! Darling I manufacture tiny chips!"
She laughed again. "All over the globe
I have my fingers in. In China, North and South
Africa, Germany, Mexico — anywhere I can I

set up my new clean factories. We make
lasers the size of atom wafers. There is
a constant increase in my annuities. I may be
dying, but I've invested well.

                               You seem so
uncomfortable — it's hot in here, isn't it? I
don't like the air conditioner, I never felt
it was one of my better inventions — oh, it
works all right I suppose but that terrible
sensation of living with all the windows closed
as if nature were laying siege — of course it
did, for a decade or two, but we've gotten
beyond that, haven't we, we've made — progress."

       She held my eyes. Sweat carved
the flesh on my back and under my breasts. The
smell returned in patterns, now pine-scented,
now something rotten, or a low sour wave of ash.
"You're not trapped, you know, you
are free to leave. You're able, mobile —"

I remembered my forms. "Oh. Disability. Your
disability is work, accident or genetically
related?" This time the laugh stayed
in her cheeks. "All," she said.
"I lost the use of my legs in Phnom Penh,
or was it in that fishing boat
off the coast of Hiroshima? A factory
explosion near Leningrad you never
read about? The Chicago doctor gave my mother
tranquilizers when she carried me. Really —
it's an act of god, don't you think?"

"Right — religion?" She stopped smiling completely.
"I used to. Very self-righteously. My children, some of them —
I tried a few ancient rituals in the last
years but I — the closer I am towards the end,
the less I believe."
                    "Still, you must have been
born into some faith?" "I was, exactly,
born into some faith. But I consider this question

an invasion of my privacy." We have our instructions.
I had to let it go but by then I thought
I was on to something.
                              "And don't you
want to know why I haven't aged?"
"Yes, but you just called me prying."
"It's my prerogative, isn't it? Anyway
it's only a trick done with mirrors. Look."
An invisible control turned the dimmer
switch. Even in the bright light she
didn't look more than thirty. Thirty and sick.

"And you want to know about *my* faith!
In 1903 when babies were thrown onto
bayonets, people in their outrage said
'To think this can happen in the 20th century!'
Everyone wants to think their age
the most modern. You are not exempt.
Here I am, your 20th century girl. Tell them
I had a wonderful singing voice, that
I was forever young."

                              On the small table
by her side there was a single stone, and she
started to roll it in her palm. "I think it's
time for you to leave." We went back
through the corridor, but now each inch
was hung with photos of politicians and
framed newspaper advertisements
for every car ever manufactured in the world.
There was a reek of sulphur, and then
fresh bread.
                              "Thank you," I said, when the
bolts were all unfastened and I could fix
on the familiar, unwavering stench of
overripe rose. "My pleasure. I'm always
glad for guests. I want to give you
a little going away present."

She put
the stone she had been fiddling with
in my hand. "A friend of mine, a child
survivor of the Warsaw Ghetto uprising,
went back to see Treblinka, she and
her mom, the last of her family. She sent me
this. I think you should have it. A
legacy, and all you had to do
was your job. Don't worry, no risk."

She wheeled the chair around
and locked the door. I put the papers in
my briefcase and stared at a cloudless sky.
The stone burns in my fist.

A Law of Physics
Saturday, March 25, 1911

One body falling alone is it's own weight
times distance.
Two bodies falling alone are their own but
if they hold hands
their weight is multiplied.

Here's a for instance:
Two girls are on a ledge.
The building is burning.
There are nets below.
The girls are young and for the purpose
of this example
thin and frightened.
It is eight stories to the ground.
The net can hold 90, 120, 150 pounds
times the distance but
holding hands
they become 11,000 pounds on impact.
The net breaks.
No one knows the price
of comfort,
how much they loved each other
and expected, by jumping,
neither to live nor die
but fly
released
from the Triangle Shirtwaist Factory.

146 workers, almost entirely Jewish and Italian women, died within 18 minutes during the Triangle Shirtwaist Factory Fire. The high death rate was attributed to not following safety and fire regulations, including the company's policy of keeping the fire doors locked to prevent employees from "sneaking out." Over 120,000 people marched in the funeral procession. This tragedy reoccurred in 1993 in a toy factory outside of Bangkok — fire, locked doors, jumping women, over 200 dead.

The promised land

I know the story
and after 40 years
they were bound to be grateful.
I've come through mountains
bordering a desert and been changed
by green, by flowering trees but
there must have been a woman
who looked at the flat, mottled scene
and realized
what a long hype the journey had been
no paradise no easy life
just work to be done
and the beginning of a sensation
that lasted millennia:
work to be done
never your own place, after all,
to do it from.

fifteen minutes from the kar kare klinic

JEWS should not live where I live
on the coast of oregon   we should move somewhere
when I was a kid
they said l.a. was safe, but it isn't anymore
not safe for kids' windows to sport menorahs
in new york where my grandmother
was an old jewish woman
a gang of white girls pushed her
into the gutter, broke her hips

they paint it on the sides of buildings
all over the states
all over the world
it keeps on reappearing
doesn't go away
every other day I clip it out of the newspapers
once we were in the flamingo cafe in new orleans
a group of highly painted secretaries were talking
—mama knows all about the jews   she dated one—

it's
easy to make this list
places where jews should not live:
in germany   in egypt   in portland
in yreka   in utah   in paris
in ghettos
outside of big cities   like skokie
in cuba   in the south
even miami isn't so great
in oakland they bait jews at their workplaces

Between 1979 and 1983, my partner and I were the only jewish lesbians on the southern oregon coast for hundreds of miles. The Kar Kare Klinic was owned by the organization its initials indicate. Shortly after this poem was written, the lone jewish tailor in town (fifteen minutes in the other direction) had his shop burned down. In 1983 we moved to oakland.

& I don't expect it's easier in uganda
new zealand any
catholic protestant muslim or hindu nation
in the soviet union
in spain algeria chile bolivia buenos aires
el salvador nicaragua cape verde
south africa canada poland
a jew should not live alone
a jew should not live with other jews
it provokes attention
a jew should not live in the native lands of others
a jew should not live in israel
jews aren't israelis, they're just immigrants
they should have stayed out
should have stayed out of boston
out of singapore and canton
they should get out of california

and we should leave southern oregon

desire, jews, casino

I
she dreams of dripping water
a flooded race track.
the bets are all
in a foreign language which
might be spanish might be hebrew she isn't sure
she hasn't studied
when her grandfather was alive
they came out to the track
like a picnic, like a baseball outing
jews like to gamble a friend says
where you find casinos
there are jews
the week in tahoe didn't go well still
she picked up the tip to
always play machines
near the doors or food lines
the house likes noisy visible scores

tonight she has an urge to get back in the car
and drive up there
the middle of the night who cares now
there's a days food in the feeder for the cat
she could go anywhere
tired of desire being attached to womyn
you can attach desire
to four of a kind to a royal flush
desire is like a leech it can fasten its mouth anywhere
it doesn't really need flesh or touch
the rough hull of a boat will do any fast car anything shiny that moves

II
was that you?
complaining about desire?
complaining about desire and being a jew?
wanting a quick risk
a way to beat the odds

wagering what you get from the culture's hate:
'o you jews are all so smart'
against your own fear of loss —
quick — watch those cards
it can be gone in a flash
or is it guilt, jew, to have even a week's worth of extra cash
here
take it, enmesh me endlessly in this drama about jews and money

about america and money about jews and america and money
the big casinos on the western lake
knowing just how much we can afford to lose
balancing loss against win
fear of money and the true sins of money
with the fear of death
of growing old in debt
fear of the knock on your door   genetic
fear of not having a bribe ready
when they come for you

III
or was it lesbians and desire?
would you start across the valley, into the sierra at midnight
because you don't live with your lover anymore
because you have no lover and you're tired of lovers
and you wish your old lovers
still wanted to touch you
wish you still wanted to touch them
wish that desire wasn't such a leech
siphoning vitality from your veins

until what's left is a collection of games
you can't bear to play
facing anyone more intimate than the dealer
the dealer doesn't know you
but she knows your face
she can see in your face desire's ash
rolling for a seven, laying a stack on twenty two
gambling is something you can do with your hands

you know it.   tonight you resist the desire
to blow it shooting craps until four
but it doesn't change the way desire has you pacing
tracing your shadows in blood
you want
to take your desire
and attach it
once and for all to belief
on something that's safe
if not as bright as a slot machine,
if not as beautiful as her face,
then you demand
to desire yourself
want to believe you can own
your own reactions

you're still that naive

IV
o midnight eye
scowling across my dreams
I have a hard time losing money to machines
though I do it now and then
waiting for the perfect chance
and even if I say
there's nothing useful in romance
if it came gleaming through the night if she smiled at me just right
I'd go

haven't I written this poem before?

it's so easy to repeat yourself in midlife
waiting for the trick the knack
the winning streak that
leads out of the casino

big belly on the road from reno

big belly rides around america
eating potato chips
enters the mountains
where she's slit branches
off sage plants
native american lesbians say
don't harvest the sacred sage
she wonders if this means
for personal use too
for the smell of it
hanging up, drying in her room
all these acres of
nothing but sage
and lizard and rock
she has sage from the last time
out on the porch but it's true
she doesn't light it as often
doesn't stop this time
so many things
that deal with smell and smoke
are traditions
this great west
is not her country
if the west is not her country
and new york is sepia memory
then she has none
she leaves the plants alone

***

waiting at home there's a message
on her answering machine:
send money to: an address:
for dykes who were run off land
in southern oregon
by organized aryans
because the dykes were jews
were jews and lesbians

run off: swastikas painted on their land
guns shot
on both sides   in the air.
big belly has been to reno and lost money
on a roll of dice
a hand of cards.

***

later big belly is on
the other side of the mountain
the potato chips are gone
when she stopped for dinner
by a nearly dry creek
there was a sound of cowbells above her
and the wind shaking alder leaves
she sat in her tank top
on a granite bolder
a fat lesbian eating the half sandwich
that came with the potato chips
thinking
what a lucky life
this is

***

in the valley there are orchards
irrigation makes this possible
she loves to travel
to make the twilight curve of earth
her habitation

big belly wishes for a minute
she had been a farm daughter
brave in the dimming smudge
under thick fruit awnings
staking out the shapes
of childhood phantoms
in that fantastic shade

***

the first time they drove by copperopolis
big belly said: copper-op-olis!
copperopolis! let's
check it out.
(you have to turn left off route four
go west into town
which is tucked into an elbow of earth
as the sierras taper down to
the great growing valley —
copperopolis the last mining village
on the map the next name
is farmington.)
but her lover said:
no. I know enough about the life
of women in small towns.
I don't have to go out of my way
to look at another one.

the women? big belly hadn't given them
the thought. she was hoping for
rock shops and mining shafts,
ma's hometown diner, a great
hardware store stocking
jeans in every size. the women?
their lives?
this time she's alone and
makes the turn. in copperopolis
there's a bar with a sign:
minors expressly forbidden.
a general store that rents videos,
two guys playing checkers
in front of the fire station,
neat little houses wide spaced,
dotted, almost, along the road
she turns around in front of the old armory:
bingo 1st and 3rd saturdays.
driving back to route four
the woman   is there
on the deck in front of the bar,
a thin white woman in a loose print dress,
opening the door.

***

across the highway,
walking down a side street,
a young couple and their labrador.
it's not just Willa Cather updated,
it's video discs and home computers,
mail order business an hour
from stockton and   women
living in rural places
with men and dogs.

***

it gets dark in the valley.
she puts a tape on to keep awake
everything poignant and damp
with the changing light
the car goes up and down
waves of land   accurately
she appears to be steering
through liquid
some golden stubble of substance
that heaves upward and subsides
burnt patchy black along its crest
then flattens to fields

glass, she thinks, but doesn't know why.
glass reminds her of love
of knowing womyn
of how many womyn
whose transparencies
she felt she could read
if not like glass
then layers of rock on an exposed ridge
each layer set down by elements
thrust up by force,
dramatic events, the record clear
if you put your mind to it
and studied striation

but you were something else entirely,
she says to a ghost in the car,
more like mud
— oh mud, how flattering —
not that kind of mud,
the kind that's left
at the bottom of strong coffee
the essence from which
everything derives flavor
then you swirl what's left
to tell the future —
something big belly could never do
no matter how many times
she looked thoughtfully
deep into the cup

***

big belly remembers an invitation
to talk to elementary school children.
—what would I say to them?
—whatever you want.

then I would talk
poetry and geography
how among the greatest gifts
is to be able to read a map
to place yourself on it
and know which roads
are the fastest
which the most absorbing

and then: the way your mother sings
or doesn't sing to you
all of that
will form layers and make you
your own place

excavate and explore
in order to find who's story
your life is telling

poem for my unborn niece

They'll say you have an aunt in california
I'll send presents
stuffed animals   an erector set
They'll say
your aunt is fat, she's a writer, she was supposed to be
the smart one in the family
but she never made much money.
I'll send you a picture   I'll be almost grey by then
and you'll swear you never saw
such a big womon   smiling
They'll say   she never married
When you're older
they'll tell you   or a cousin will whisper
at someone's bat mitzvah
Your aunt in california — she's a lesbian
It will seem mysterious, dangerous, eccentric,
an ancient shadow, a story
grownups know the end of and they won't tell
I'll write you a letter
I'll say it's true   I'm a fat lesbian,
and I'll tell you the stories of womyn
living mysteriously   in a dozen countries
if you tell me yours

come visit me

the real fat womon poems

I.
I went to get a glass of water
and was overtaken by grief
grief at the kitchen sink
womyn's grief
for the life that vanishes
hot water and grease
for the hundred fears
about what we eat
and what size we are
and whether standing,
with soap lining the creases of our hands,
hurts our backs or feet
and if that's our fault.
It was dark in your kitchen.
You had been complaining
about your body,
bitter attacks on the new swells
that define your belly and hips.
And I said
so why don't you hack yourself to pieces?
And you said I wish I could.
When I got to the sink
I couldn't turn the faucet on.
The white porcelain dull
under the light from the yard
couldn't speak
my back to you
my back against the world
grief at the kitchen sink
a womon's drama
the fat womyn's fight
the silence we were born into
catching us.

II.
Will the real fat woman please stand up?
We want to take a good look at you.
Don't you trust us to look?
What is it you think will come to focus,
where do you think we'll begin?
With your double chin, the roundness of your cheeks,
the width of your upper arms—there
does the flesh ripple, or are they full?
Do they bulge, are they smooth?
Where are your stretch marks?
Did you gain weight fast or slow?
Do you eat a lot at once or
do you eat a little all day long?
We all know a fat woman is
what she eats.
Can we watch you eating?
You must be hiding something
in your flesh,
is it rage or sex?
C'mon, we're your friends,
we just care about you and we want to see
where the fabric hugs the expanse of your stomach
the rolls at your waist
the fat that collects in pockets on your upper back.
What kind of stomach do you have?
High and round, or does it slip, slowly,
towards your knees, do your nipples
scratch the top of your pants?
Do your pants fit?
When your clothes are too tight
do you feel like you're
exploding out of them
into the street
and all you want to do is
get out of sight?

III.
Asshole, asshole,
I can answer for myself,
you don't know anything

You ask these questions
as if I were an interesting specimen
as if I wasn't you
Who did this to us?
And what makes you think
I would ever trust you?

IV.
There is being fat,
and there is eating.
There is eating, and
then there's the food.
There is fat and
there is aging
There is aging
and there is disability.

None of these things
are the same things
though they are used,
often, interchangeably.
Who did that?
Who did that to us?
And with each of these words
is the word: ugly.
Even with the word
eating, the word ugly is paired
by womyn
in north america
in the late 20th century.

V.
Now there are politics
for these things.
Unpopular politics,
but there are some.

We live in a country
that consumes,
that needs consumption
to continue consuming,

and what gets consumed
are the resources and the lives
of dark skinned and poor people,
the lives of women in sweatshops,
of women carrying rocks on their heads
in india to build american hotels.
We saw a lot of newsreels in the '60s.
Some of us stopped watching the news
but the news doesn't change.
Even if I choose carefully,
don't want my "major purchases"
to contribute to the evil
done to people in soweto,
some woman in a factory
compromised her eyes or her lungs
her back or her labor
for my computer
for your vcr
for the stereo, hell, for the music.
When did we let ownership
purchase our analysis?
Consider it: they don't have to buy us out
we pay them.

It would be nice to have a target
an easy simple target   who could take
some of this unease
about our consumerism.
The fat womon, she'd do.
She moves slow, and she's wide.
It's her who starves children
across the globe
it is her hideous appetite
that makes us ashamed to be americans.
All those fat cats living off the fat of the land
we don't have access to,
the fat cats who are
lean men in limousines.
We call them fat
because we have been taught
that fat means eating

means consuming
means taking the rights to what is not yours
and these things which are not the same things
become the fat woman's fault
it's a shame she's so out of control.
We hope she stays indoors.

VI.
Oh, those politics
I thought you were going to talk
about the other stuff.
What other stuff?
You know, the stuff about the diet industry
and the stuff about women
hating ourselves
wanting to hack off parts of our bodies
sew our mouths shut
pull out our intestines
suck the fat with syringes
wrap ourselves in constricting plastics
take drugs that make our hearts race
race away from us.

VII.
In the zoo they have signs
polar bears may weigh up to half a ton.
A girl is reading the sign out loud.
"Wow!" she says.
We are standing there admiring the polar bear
who is doing back flips in her pool.

If they stuck a sign on the human race
and said members of this species
occasionally reach a weight of 1,000 pounds
but weights in the range of 1-400 are most common
would that help?

VIII.
Saturday afternoon, doing errands,
I catch pieces of a radio speech
on power relations.
A woman is talking about
the pleasures of mutuality,
not power over, but power with.
How we might better express power to our benefit
by touching and being touched
hugging and being hugged
feeding and being fed.
On the radio she said
it is a good and mutual pleasure
to feed and be fed.
I catch my breath.
Is it still possible
to transmute
the power relations
around eating
so that there is
mutual pleasure left?

IX.
I am a fat womon
I can speak for myself
but what would I say to you?
Why do I think I need
to tell you how much
sugar, how much meat
I eat in a day, in a year?
Why do I think I need
to tell you how often I go swimming
or how, if my feet hurt,
it's a problem anyone can have,
fat or thin, why
do I want to tell you
the statistics about dieting
the fact that it's thin people
who suffer most from heart disease.
And why do I think
no matter what I tell you

you will think I'm lying.
Unless I tell you I spend all my time
eating chocolate cake in front of the tv.
That I eat three chocolate cakes a day
and two six packs of coke
in between my six meals
and I get up in the middle of the night
to eat pancakes.
You'd believe that, wouldn't you?
And I remember
when they called all
fat womyn fools.

X.
I am a lucky fat woman.
If I lie in bed and have a fantasy
about eating six chocolate cakes
of being fed six chocolate cakes
by six fat womyn
who are admiring my six new rolls of flesh
I can get   pleasure from my fantasy
and know that it's resistance
to this ridiculous persistence of shame
thrown at me.
I can get up and go about my business
without too much pain,
struggle with how I eat like every womon I know—
does wheat give you arthritis,
do the chemicals they inject into apples
give us cancer in our apple juice?
How do I balance my years of anger and deprivation
with my desire to eat what's "good for me"?
How do I know, when they say it's good,
it isn't this year's medical fashion hoax,
another way to hate fat womyn?
I like to eat.
I like to feed other womyn
and be fed
when I can bear that intimacy.
I like intimacy when I can bear it —
when I can trust you.

I have appetites in my mind
that I cannot express in my body
at least not yet,
I work on it.

But I hear what's been said
when I look in the mirror
and I'll be honest
I have the words fat and ugly
paired in me.
The pairing of the words
makes me turn away faster
than what I actually see.
I touch myself and I
feel good beneath my hands
Sometimes I have lovers sometimes
they enjoy my body and enjoy me
enjoying theirs.
When I don't have lovers
I feel good beneath my hands.
This makes me a very lucky fat woman.
If I believe the evidence,
the testimony of other fat womyn,
it makes me an extraordinary fat woman
and that's a tragedy.

XI.
A very thin womon, disabled,
tells me how she spent a day crying
because she was afraid to get
on cross country skis
afraid of her own fragility,
afraid to be physical in the world.
She tells me because I would understand
and I do.
I know womyn who are fat who vomit.
I know womyn who are thin who vomit.
Womyn close to me hate their bodies,
womyn who know everything in this poem already
hate their bodies.

Womyn hate our bodies.
We have been working for justice, out of love,
in the different ways we understand it,
for years, in a hundred movements.
We have been going to twenty therapies
bodyworkers and twelve-step groups—
And remember we're lesbians
we lust for one another in our good moments
we tickle and rub
and   we   hate   our   bodies
What keeps you from understanding
what you do to me?
What did they pay you to do this to yourself?
Who does this to us?
Where is our courage?
And what happened to our resistance
to our simple stubbornness
not to let our enemy win
not to let our enemy win inside us.

&. only
    light in the forest
    fog deep over sea
    width and height of redwoods
    song of spider
    song of leaf on leaf in the mountains
    a thousand green shadows
    moving

    the things that heal
    without thought of healing

    the world that signs itself
    & has no other need for speech

After reading *The Queen of Wands*

"If not in every generation, then in every other, the sons rise up against their mothers and entomb them, still alive, in walled-in rooms."

— Inez Riverfingers

Listen, I've seen Helen
we're in the middle
of that battle now
dykes stole her
from a family house
Who do you think
the damn prince is anyway?
One of us,
sneaking past the guards,
an ordinary lesbian
who wants a beer
with the queen.
Helen is not her name
her eyes are black
she is not blond
the story was a lie
from the beginning
and it's time
to stop passing lies on.
She has fat arms
and when she raises them
in smoky rooms
snapping her fingers
leaning into the dance
her body rippling
makes waves
where hearts sink

and rise again
renewed by challenge
ready for war
at the walls of our city
ready for her
ready for ourselves at last

Some notes on the nature of the bad queen

The bad queen lived in
a cut glass palace at
the bottom of a lake.
She commanded bubbles,
and the bubbles
never had the nerve to break.

Now try to remember her seriously.
The point about the bad queen is
she is always too beautiful too exotic
too vain too arrogant too greedy
too pushy. Too much.
Demanding and impossible to touch.

When you dream about her
you fear she is your mother
or your sister, and she will
deny you in your hour of need.

The bad queen betrays women.

She is always the Other.

She changes costume to meet
our necessity to name her
Vashti, Helen —
it's hard to remember
good queens, isn't it?
The queen has no peer.
She's alone in the palace.
She has spies who want her favor
but her lover is always a secret.

Who loves the bad queen?
The cold, the ruthless,
the isolate woman —

whose country is this?

She stares in the mirror.
No one brings her daisies
or sends postcards.
She has no living mother.
There's a rumor
she turned her daughter into a frog.
She has been initiated
into some mystery
but no one ever says how
or with whom.

You're afraid
she'll take it upon herself
to initiate you
without your consent
without telling you the rules —
she's the queen
after all.

Who would choose
to be the bad queen's lover?

Centuries have stripped her
of all ornament.
There is only the will to power
that comes across
as self-obsession.

Once she had at least
control of the women's quarters,
but the women
are decimated
hiding in separate tiny houses.

Maybe the bad queen had a vision.
Maybe she had only desire.
Maybe she was battered or tricked
into submission.
Maybe she left behind
a secret manuscript
we have yet to discover

naming every act
every choice

the passion she had
to touch
each one of us

the bright fury
with which she hungered
to illuminate her lands.

A fool for love

It's harder now, to organize,
than in my 20s.   Then
when I said I wanted to do it for lesbians
if there was a question
the question was
why do it for lesbians, who are they?
I was sure of my answer
of my love and pride
my pride in love

But now I fear
when I say I want us
who so clearly need each other
to speak every phrase of that need —
I want journeys with womyn
I can depend on, who can depend on me

I fear
the answer will be:
o that old thing

And no one wants to be a fool for love

Redwoods gutted by fire and ax
still grow
Where one redwood is destroyed
a ring of young trees sprout
redwoods have shallow roots
they need these circles
where root holds fast with root

after everything that's happened
because of everything that's happened

I want to imagine a world
in which we thrive
where difference engages us
and root holds fast with root

oakland: february 1991, 1 a.m.

Put me in mind of my harbor,
the easy romance of my luck.
The taste is bitter, the moon is frayed.
They say I know what I'm doing
but I whistle to myself:
the jig is up.

I've lived through enough wars in comfort
to know that living comfortably through wars means
nothing
is only circumstance.
Somewhere tonight there's an iraqi dyke who
believes in herself who takes what she's given
and makes do,
who loves womyn and her own power
to accomplish, to hide, to get by, to create,
to make a life she thinks her mother can't imagine
and that lesbian might be blown to bits
before I get to the end of this
page

At the start of this war Evelyn called me up
raved and grieved
all the wars she'd seen —
at seventy-nine, she can describe war after war
her family in israel   her grandchildren in danger
her heart in danger of
remembering the twentieth century
miserable egos   lousy mistakes
that rage across our planet
— now I don't think the salk vaccine was worth it
the telephone, the automobile.

So this is it: I live through wars.
I live in a country that kills all over the globe and never
has a bomb dropped within it's shores and I get to tell
the girls who come after

how a womon's life can be full of personal happiness,
rich with work and friendship while
human beings are vaporized with her taxes
and she she's up at 1 a.m. again
                              watching another war

Trying to understand Rosebud

The first thing a revolutionary has to know:
                              don't get caught
They teach this
even in the boy's camps.
                    Perhaps you thought: *those wimps.*

Maybe you didn't
spend enough time
with the womyn
who add: If it's worth dying for
                    then live.
                    Avoid macho posturing.
                    Do the work.
                    Hope is patience, and belief.

          Or maybe you dismissed us: *Are those virtues?*

I'm employed by the newspaper.
I drive home through berkeley after midnight.
The night of the day you died
someone's overturned a huge garbage container
blocking a lane. On telegraph avenue
police have set up barricades, stop
every young black man for questioning.

This is it: garbage in the streets
an excuse for the police to exercise
their power, *their* beliefs.

The newspapers have interviews.
Aside from your friends
who are dismissed casually

Rosebud Denovo, a woman in her twenties, was killed by berkeley, california police in
August 1992. She had broken into the residence of the chancellor of the university of california, armed with a machete. She was protesting the university's decision to make People's
Park into volleyball courts. Everyone had been evacuated and she was cornered in a bath-
room when she was killed.

no one cares. Or they're sorry
for the chancellor, or mrs. chancellor
or innocent freshmen, this rude introduction
to the fearful circus of berkeley.

No one can image a woman
so full of anger and purpose
she'd go with a knife and machete
into the chancellor's house screaming:
                        no more abuse of power
                        no more hierarchy of privilege
                        there's a class war on the streets of the city
                        and you live here serene, saying
                        let them eat volleyball
                        no more

We read in the newspapers
you were always angry
fought school principals, police,
learned the language of pipe bombs,
lived on candy bars and pepsi.

My lover says: I can identify
with her rage —
she did what I feel inside me,
I've just been socialized out of it.

A woman who could not bear authority.
Who saw power as exploitation.
        — it's for your own good   you'll understand someday
        you'll have your turn
        be a good girl   learn your place   accept —

                Fuck you.
                I don't have to take this.
                No one should take this.
                Pay attention: no one should take this.

                Our compliance is imposed upon us by force.

                See?

talk radio

all night america is talking chatting rattling on
to an audience of insomniacs night workers and those
who dial into 24-hour talk show hosts
arguing about prisoners of war
it's hard to know which war they're talking about
these are long nights   I put my ears to the window
I can hear dead writers, the last ones before electronics
the ones who remembered tablets   who took notes in pencil
whose eyes weren't burned by video screens
who didn't have that hum that plugged in noise
haunting their line
all night the line is scratching itself down by the railroad tracks
it seems so strange that goods still move mechanically
hauled onto railroad cars and trucks having to roll
to their destinations while the rest of us wait
for delivery   unconvinced
about what we get   is it real   perishable
did it come from sweatshop loading docks
hanging around with seasonal laborers and death?
disembodied words sling around my ears
now I close my ears and senses up
stuff them with the cheap tricks of binary languages
ones and zeros are the sums of our calculus
we have no time for the treaties to be negotiated no time
to be treated right it doesn't follow   once you're
part of the matrix there is no self   only the digit
this is the 21st century struggle   to resist
it's easy in the global village to manipulate
you can't keep the games from kids
can't keep people from aiming their opinions into the air
there's no sky to look at out here
well — a little sky — an old moon mounting the night in slivers
a passé rainbow shuddering between its gray wrappers
the creek swells up with rain   a few spring peepers left
it's enough for most of us   most of us aren't deep in the forest
only women running in gym shoe advertisements yelling
— I believe in mass transit, I believe in howling at the moon —
advertising is our dinner

in the end they'll send us bright cloth through replicators
the cloth will be printed in the shape of sneakers
in the shape of cellular telephones in the shape of our lovers
here's your and yours and yours
america is swollen with science fiction fantasy at night
with horror movies and real time rapists
guys down the street hanging by the fence trading drugs
it seemed so obvious the government did this
that the government floods the people they want to control
with available drugs and sets them at war
20 years ago the day after kent state during vietnam
my campus swam in reds, later
someone said: but maybe you were reaching out for them
you wanted to be sedated you wanted to be calmed
no I just noticed   and listened
I've seen plenty of mothers and the mothers say
don't baby don't   listen to your elders   believe in yourself
but the government is always more seductive:
here is the sweetness of war we give it to you complete
you don't even have to get shipped overseas
this crossfire hits us every one
I know a prison from a city street but
a guard in a suit is just as mean

back at the womyn's commune
it's not possible to write word by word anymore
fit one word against the next
joined at the seam clean no metal screws
just the planed wood fit   the little wonders of the craft of it
it's gone we don't have time it's on us all   the women know it
most of them wanna drag their guys along want to   have to   make alliances
it's been like this forever only   less urgent   more urgent   less
my friend the writer tells me at the end of
the 19th or maybe the 10th century it was
exactly like this, a great crowding and fear of death
of overwhelming technologies pestilence flood
earthquake tornado   shook every conversation
many perished and for them it was the end of the world
but for me it's the end of the day another day in oakland
I turn off the radio

american wounds

North dakota/canadian border
by the side of the road:
a rock carved along its natural line
in the shape of a buffalo
covered with trash
shoved tight into a wire cage.

On the historical marker:
"this sacred object
was moved from its original site"

Anasazi

If I were a place
I would be that indistinct area on the map
somewhere in utah, northern arizona, eastern oregon
succor creek   adobe canyon   lost mine trail
two, three hundred miles from the interstate
a ribbon of ink thru a green patch
the line for the river wider than the road
you could drive right into me
but you wouldn't know till you got there
it was where you wanted to go
you probably wouldn't choose this direction
you probably know already how long it will take
to get from santa fe to las vegas from
cheyenne, wyoming to boise, idaho
a couple hours leeway for a cup of coffee
or a detour mapped by the triple-a

I am a red and black sand cliff lit
with copper afternoon sun
great horned owls have made nests in
the indentations of my width
the river carves me   I am
huge, elemental material   lapped and lathed
until I gleam, until I reveal
the secrets of my accretions

Where the river changed course
after flood last season
there's a field of quartz-bearing rock
crystals just under the dried mud

The Anasazi, the ancient ones, lived in what is now the u.s. southwest. They disappeared around 1250, leaving behind cities, religious sites, astronomical systems — but no message that we can understand about where or why they went.

I am equally pleased with crystal,
sage brush, cottonwood,
full of caves and burrows, capable
of feeding deer, lizards, rattlesnakes —
and there are deer, lizards rattlesnakes
eating and feeding me.

There is no reason to build a town here
my crystals are too irregular and small
to support industry
I feel abundant, fertile, but unable
to provide cash crops
Too many centuries of wind erratic rain
hard winters my river sustains my ecology but
wouldn't hold a barge.
I was a sacred place, once, where Anasazi womyn
came to bleed and meditate
you can see the smoke from their fires still
on the lips of some of my caves
and inside, walls with the mark of their stones
the shapes they made of their thoughts and intentions
to remind them next season
to explain later, to their daughters,
where they were going
when they left so suddenly

I miss the Anasazi
but there is always some conversation
in my canyon owl to mouse
lizard to stone river to hawk
deer to deer rattlesnake to bones
hiss and turn, round and flat sounds
that keep me sharp in great heat,
that can sing me to sleep in ice and cold
I don't mind the dreams   when I wake

All the maps have changed
new womyn are on the distant roads
and my own shoulders have a new slope
which I'm pleased to discover

Two hundred miles off the interstate,
seventy six miles on the road between nolo and burns,
pass county marker 567, turn left onto dirt, twenty seven miles
of pitted gravel, 13 dirt along the edge of a cliff,
down into my valley

If the road doesn't slide
if the river doesn't cover it
if the snow melts this year
if you don't bust an axle in a pit
you could drive right into me

I'd share my secrets
I love the way I look,
decked out in seasons, animals, sparse green, the
russet, black, gold, tan stripes ragged
through my forms
and I love to look at the womyn
who come through me
though in this time, even those who come
look quickly, are still
in a hurry

I stay slow beneath the weather's quick costumes
it's as dangerous to believe in change as it is foolish
to think things stay the same
I know I'm rugged though I don't feel rugged to myself
I feel smooth and continuous
and I cant tell you
how much I miss the Anasazi.

Woodpeckers

Three times since the eclipse I've seen
red-headed woodpeckers.
In the bird book with its shiny plates
there is no "red-headed woodpecker,"
the closest match is "acorn."
One morning we woke early from noise —
three perched on Linnea's house.
Acorn planters, they use
an intermediate object
to get what they need.
Each acorn they place in a branch,
under the eaves, is a seed home.
They farm for bugs, their own crop,
where first light reaches
the pitched roof in the clearing.

Today I sit alone, reading —
a womon writes "faith" "divinity."
I am studious and quiet.
Faith in what? divinity from where?
I remember grappling with this
before, alone, a child standing by a lake
or ocean — who is the queen of the sabbath?
Is there an intelligence that guides
reincarnation? Is there more
than science in the orbit
of our random planet,
so unlike the veils of hydrogen
that trail between stars?

Those are the regular questions.
We answer by our station —
a womon close to her mother
will take her mother's faith.
A wandering womon will answer
as is common among those
with whom she stays or

she will travel toward those
whose answer suits her.
She will widen whatever space she finds
according to the custom of her times.
Push a little here, interpret there,
like store bought clothes that never fit,
we make do. We wear the faith
we can afford.

Reverence, observance, deity, wonder,
awe, praise, heritage, spirit:
this impulse we hold to be
filled with the presence of the world,
and through that saturation
to lose the boundary of self
gathered up
in that-which-is-great, that-beyond-us
which still remembers our name.

The woodpecker interrupts me. Tick, thack,
tick tick until I look. Without my glasses
its margins blur. I hold still, struggle
for focus. The woodpecker walks thoughtfully
along a dead aspen reclining in a hemlock's arms,
considering each peck. I want a sharp view
but when I get back with my glasses it's gone,
only her "tick thack" somewhere in the woods.

Naturalists must wait like this, patient
in the quest. A footprint, a branch,
any sign of what they stalk and they stay,
making notes, preparing to photograph
an appearance — someone pays
for photographs, for clear plates in bird books.
Naturalists and rabbis have a lot in common.
Someone pays them to wait
for inspiration, for proofs
that there is still hope on the planet, still
nature and creation.

The rest of us are lucky if we have a little time
an occasional holiday
where we see a bird we've never seen before.
Where our questions, our mother's questions,
have time to expand in the air
before they disappear again over the dry ridge.

Poem for the protection of my loved ones
for Tryna, going into surgery

The world turns and shivers.
I put my finger on the warm pulse
hushing up my neck I speak
into the telephone   surgery at 8:30   yes
I remember the emergency room
Does sending energy depend
on knowing the receiving terminal?
I have seen the faces of many womyn
after surgery   I know yours by heart

By heart: inside my veins where friendship
accretes   and rebuilds the body we
think is ours I find your face   with ease

If I send my energy back to us
walking a long redwood trail
on the oregon border eight years ago
will that energy break its barrier and find you
lying on a bed of cattails in a hospital corridor
laughing because you're safe   safe:

everything heals you   the world you
thought you would never make
fills the wound with soft herbs and
lesbians are everywhere   our hands
never stop moving   even
when one of us falls or dies   we form
around her absence   clotting scabbing
fixing the skin that contains us   and tonight
I wish— the moon is just past full and I
wish on the world
I wish on our belief on our possibility
on our enormous grief as well as our courage

to protect you to find you here
protecting me
wherever a blade might go.

Take anything
for Dolphin

I
Experience was supposed to be our friend,
and we learn
but as we learn we get worn away.
Any smooth rock on the beach
will skip and gleam but
brought home
heaped on our table
we wonder at its dullness
the day forgotten.

She was smiling there was water
the reflection of light on water
she handed me a stone
or I picked up a stone when
I was on the beach away from her
and saw the bodies of dead birds
twisted into kelp.
I thought beach rocks
would help me remember
everything: love and mortality
the glistening of the air as I turned towards her.
Now I live alone in oakland
with a pile of stones.

II
In a city gallery we find
kelp twined into baskets by artists.
At least it finally has a use.
The city blows sand
in the eyes of our memory
stings the pleasure off our rural shores.

A day at the beach:
girls use kelp for whips

they pretend to slash each other
or they don't pretend
they do
the children wash bloody ankles in salt water.

III
But we had nights, didn't we?
Fires in a sand pit
and the girls danced for the joy of it
I walked alone
watching the moment the tide turned
feeling the pull of gravity
the slight shift of motion at sea.
Then you were there, guiding me back
to the womyn, the fire
holding out your hand
and in your hand
all your favorite stones and beads.
Take anything,
you said to me.

These things:

my heart is broken
my heart is wide open

my heart is broken
the way land is broken
after earthquake, heavy flood.
pastures still invite the eye
but lie treacherous with mud,
sinkholes, sudden fissures.
hillsides erode in graceful terraces
that threaten to slide.
the landscape's cut up
with barren inexplicable places
but still
offering shade
beneath almond trees
where womyn might rest and feast
on islands in that shattered geography
as difficult to get to
as they are dangerous to leave.

A deliberate slowing

It rained for weeks

I've seen the nature film:
where the cracked river bed floods
and a frog startled into life
bursts from mud

There are creatures that persevere
dried and patient
underground for years

Time lapse photography
has changed our imaginations

Quick   I am kissing you
streets are wet, full
of fallen fruit blossoms you
motion me close to your breast
the ground saturates, reservoirs fill

Then
sudden relentless quality of heat
a moment of still uncertainty
before all the small creatures
burrow backwards in their land
towards the cool, unseen place
ready to wait
a season   a generation
for cloudburst

At first pushing the pulse back hurts
but we learn
a deliberate slowing of the heart
insures survival
in the harshest loops
of our cycle

the thing we long for

the ticking is rocking away in the night
with our hearts half curdled and the moon not right
and all of the animals twitching and spry
to get their own chances for whatever lies

                                              beyond the rise

dark under fog
reflecting only the black sparks in the stream
dark at the back of the yard

and this quiet starts us baying
whenever we have no idea what we mean

there's a shape out there
a quantity
we know it   we gnash our teeth in our dreams
all elusive, and still concrete

we don't find the words
we don't find the thing though we dig in the soft sand
we've got maps in hand marking the tree stump where it was hid
we know its circumference
its jingle   its absence of shine
its weight

                but damn if we can see her face

Blood letting
for Sheila Gilhooly

She could only hear the blood in her head.
She could hear it quite loudly.
Moving up there.
The doctors say it's impossible
for blood to make that sound, their
procedures are clean, electrical, convenient.
There is no blood
when these procedures are
in effect. No pain to feel. She must
be fantasizing pain.
And that's reason enough
to wire her up again.

Nevertheless the pain is real.
She does the simple thing, cuts
her wrists deep to let the blood.
Then
everyone is afraid.

This is the wrong place to be walking
when you need to bleed.
There is proof that blood needs to be shed,
to be cupped, to be sucked, to be given up but
we do not accept this proof.

Womyn bleed to death internally,
the bones of madness
stuck in our throats too polite to scream
help me

Written after seeing the slideshow *Still Sane*, from the remarkable book by the same name,
by Persimmon Blackbridge and Sheila Gilhooly, published by Press Gang, Vancouver, BC.

It's everywhere, not just on the wards.
Moments, days of pain that have no outlet
no ritual, not so much as a mark in our soft flesh

I have been hurt, the dream cries.
The shape of the dream itself bleeds into sleep,
until sleep is changed.
Then you may need to hit a vein.
You may need to howl through blood,
smear your body across the landscape: your room,
your job, your lover's face, someone's grave.
The monthly blood hardly satisfies
the way blood teeming from a sharp slice
in your arm might   if the occasion was right

I know what suicide is   and this
has nothing to do with it   the womon
has no desire to die

but live in ritual,
open the blood hope
where suffering
has been denied

My mother's gifts

My mother still stands in the corridor
writing letters on the institution walls
sealing pieces of plaster in envelopes
that are slow in the overseas mail reaching me
I tear them open
plaster covers the floor.
My regrets pock the dust
the way meteors attack the moon
no atmosphere to stop them.

My mother brought me to the door of the locked ward
She wanted to   touch me
        You   are my only daughter
I didn't let her   I didn't wave goodbye   I was thirteen
eleven years ago last october at midnight   I forced my mother
away
There are certain events one always remembers.
Later on there may be other confessions
glossy and useless as the sunday comics.
                                    All these years
the only presents she sends
are sweaters:
when she travels, she remembers
her daughter lives in the north alone
She doesn't want me
to be cold.

my mother used to have that dream

We were standing in her kitchen
the kitchen of the womon who
had been my lover
I was trying to leave
She didn't want me to go
I didn't want to go
but I could see no other
way to be
She could not move toward me
she was crying
she said it wasn't that she
didn't want to, she didn't know
what stopped her
my need wasn't strange or
unreasonable to her still
she could not respond to me
unless we were having this scene
she said she dreamed she could not
move, she opened her mouth
and no words came out
I said
my mother used to have that dream
she was standing on a beach
watching her children drowning
swept away on the surf
and she couldn't move to save them
she opened her mouth, like you,
but she could not scream

I am my mother's daughter
I am out beyond the breakers
in dangerous water
the womon on the beach
sees me go down
tangled in kelp, exhausted
or a huge wave
catches me in its break

I see her standing there
fixed   unable to swim toward me
unable to make a sound,
neither cry for help nor encouragement

I have been lost at sea
to many womyn in just this way
including my mother
one minute they are thinking
everything is well with us
and the next
I'm a ghost

What they never see is how I
surface on the other side
of the wave
paddling slowly
for another coast

waking: the last line of a dreamt poem:

to return to
as to yourself

a dream about the traveler
ashamed of her passport
and afraid to travel without it

who do you go to?
where do you return?

about to set out for the island
for my mother's home

I want to return from my mother's house
with something other than ache and absence

the journey hands us over
traveling against the grain   as if
we are explorers and
everything we touch is new, new
just for us
the world of insight uncolonized
the landscape of meaning unharmed
by the flush of our terrible excitement

then wonder gives way to recognition:
but this
is my own house
my own little backyard
my own struggle

a hand on my shoulder:
a face saying: glad you're back
unexpected   inevitable
to return to
as to yourself

We change each other

I am a womon of opaque windows
set at oblique angles
a face in each one
covered with nylon stocking or grey crepe.
You know
this image.
I close the shutters of my body
one by one
— let no light in this house
and don't poke around in my vagina either.
You refuse to take it
seriously.
Suddenly I turn a corner
in the twenty fourth corridor
where all the windows are made
of polished black amber
and the sills are volcanic ash.
There you are
you've brought your bright red pillow
you've got your feet up against the window
and have hung your goddam plants.
Doesn't that look nice?
No I say get out
I may love you in meadows
but this is queer palace
there isn't room for two.
Effortlessly you unhinge the locked blinds.
There that's better these vines need sun.
Come on now — we have to live where we can.
I start to weep
and you pull me to your breasts
with tough hands.

Tell me a story

"Let's say we have a mystery guest
she has turquoise skin—"
I lie in the shallow of your armpit
waiting for the story to begin but really
I want to tell you how I lived in a turquoise house once
the only turquoise house on the block
because my mother was in the hospital and my father
had it painted as a surprise,
how shocked, aggrieved my mother was
how I wanted to be like my father,
paint a whole house in colors no one else used
for fun, for the hell of it.
I want to ask now that you've met my father
and you can see how like him I modeled myself,
witting and unwilling,
do you still love me
for my simple lesbian ingenuity?
Do you love me as one-who-comes-from-a-family
as well as for this fierce orphan independence
I take? Quick, I want to say, tell me quickly —

We were all at dinner and the two of you were talking law
and I saw the way the boats moved up and down
on their moorings, the way the bay darkens as night
infuses the water
—your sex darkens sometimes that way
from a change in the atmosphere that appears
to come from underneath —
that's what I want to say: the surface can shine from
some ordinary or even horrible thing happening
and that happening, which we attribute to ourselves,
may not be ourselves at all,
but we walk around pleased with us, strut, almost,
convinced we're originals, while we mirror our families or place,
not even having the grace of precise observation.

I am quiet and looking at you
— your sex darkening from a change in atmosphere
that seems to come from underneath...
"Comfortable?" you ask me
and I shift my weight until my face is as close
to your scent as I can make it be
cinnamon and sweat,
some dry, rusty, calming smell and the smell
of coconut oil from your neck,
"Yes," I say, "comfortable.
Tell me a story."

Carrying the Ark
For Susan L.

You take everything seriously.
My flesh is in your palm   your face is hot
and above me. On the couch
you are young,15, then 25, silly, pulsing
with found love   but in bed
you age the forty desert years
want narrows your cheeks
while your fingers lengthen and you insist,
insist on repeating my fantasies until
we are chanting words, mine, yours
— more — a wail of longing and disbelief
through which we make our way
toward faith, that breathing arc faith is,
arches from precipice to ledge, my hands banding
your wrists while you shudder and wave, ark
in which the surviving remnant is carried,
the sacred words are kept.

You remember
everything that has happened since the diaspora,
the burning synagogues, the dogs of selma.
You cannot watch movies about brutality,
you must have tenderness now   real
tenderness   and sex has to be this unexpected yard
marvelous with hue and bloom;
beneath the canopy
where we have stopped to rest
messages spelled in tangles by the wild hard root.

Sex has to be
your hands in that dirt   has to be

The ark is the cabinet in which the torah is kept. Traveling by foot, an ark may be carried
fastened to poles which rest on the shoulders.

the dirt turning over, dark, reliable, origin of ritual,
our lost holidays coming back
succhos, purim, pesach —
the invocation of a hunger that spreads,
joining the drifting continents
of childhood and middle-age   and you
are so serious, cupping the promise
as I cup your face —
we write over the sheets, the dirt,
the page, we turn and have at last
the secret of sex
scrolling back my skin to let you seek
your covenant in me.

Alchemy

the wizard opens her doorway.
sometimes there are flowers.
a peach would be nice.
but out of season.
anything out of season
is not in reason.
so she says.
what happens in that doorway
anyway?
I say I can see it.
the wizard doesn't say anything.
any fruit I give her
she changes
how does she change it?
well just the way I would
by eating.

great barrier reef

night diving
on the great barrier reef
sex is
to approach a sleeping fish
tenderly
to find her nook
and pull her out
press your eye to her lidless eye
stare down her knowledge
of the depth

without startling
without waking her

even my eyes become mouths

Forgetting what I'm about
your naked belly appears to me
wet from the bath
as you walk around   and I
am laying you down
with a palm on each of your sides
until full & pushed
you open
the pomegranate, the fig
got nothing on this   as
I press my face
into the hot bowels of you
and even my eyes
become mouths
to drink that juice

like paradise

your body is like paradise to me
not the stormy paradise of adam and eve
fruit hanging everywhere
and serpents steaming up the trees
this
is simpler   it
doesn't hiss
only whispers
your scent across the sheets
on occasional wednesdays
your flesh unwrapping the night
moving towards, away, towards
my hand cupping a fold of your belly
pulling me up to you before
the alarm starts its last song
this
sturdy, unmentioned time
where my eye pressed to your heart
photographs a landscape
of thick, vital womyn
a world where love
does
change everything

Bowls — A Series
for Susan Jill

The Gift

I.

Containers for contexts:

Glass for childhood
Wood for what's broken & what can be grown
The pottery of our bodies
Metal that sings at our touch
Sky that holds us & comes next

Patient hours go into these shapes
and I find it's
not simply a question of creating bowls
into which I can give

but how I hold
what's come to me

I used to be hungry for the poetry
of middle and old age
what happens   what happens
when womyn take their own shape
become the body of their experience

Now I am a middle aged woman
seeking forms that can speak for me
in their delicacy and intent

Outside acacia bend in the rain
there are glacial bowls cut into rock
there are bowls woven from
willow bark so fine and tight
they do not leak

I collect these contemplations
but their urgency frightens me

I often seek electronic consolation
Take me away
from what I know

I clasp my hands
and press my knuckles hard into my teeth
I don't like to wet my face like this

Am I cracked pottery
crizzled glass
meshed steel

    How many throws does it take
    to feel satisfied
    with the shape?

  Alone in the studio
  I paint tiny designs, teach myself intaglio
  shatter the day's work, melt the pieces down
  but gradually I name the bowls
  and give each their place

II.

These are my bowls
hold them with me

All this starts
in what our own love
can & cannot carry

I realize how I may appropriate
your work   saying
you can do it this way &
if you don't want to do it this way   just
see it can be done
take heart   start to do it on your own

Too many voices tell you what to do —
if you need a way to trust your strength,
the curve of your grace holding your own gifts

if you need to know
it's up to you
what to offer and what to take
find you can be filled without glut
share without being consumed

that's yours to do and
mine only to encourage

not knowing what to give you
turning 40
I choose to give
what I know how to make

Bowls of words

Glass

We come with our fairytales complete

        glass shatters
        we cannot keep it safely in our homes
        slivers of glass pierce the heart
        glass   or ice
        the snow queen scoops the child
        who lives removed
        from the broken pieces
        of a brittle childhood

She lives where everything is danced
pretty   under a dome of glass
nothing can change the seasons of artifice

It's a story we tell about our mothers
     how our mothers
couldn't hold us   couldn't embrace
the round pliant shapes of their bodies
            withheld

We know this story so well we're inclined to see it everywhere
the shape of earth heaped up in mounds or
any round ornament   attracts and repels us

we feel trapped behind
walls of industrial glass

        dreaming we can see the moving crowd through our case
        but cannot reach or be reached toward
        glass so thick no voice can penetrate

            what kind of glass is that?

A friend says   remember how they told you
it was only old glass that warps and shimmers?

Not true she said
they lie about everything   glass is liquid   all glass keeps moving
any huge plate will show the shift in motion
it's just slow
we can't measure it in days
                              This glass

                    flows into bowls
          and the bowls are carved with fantastic geometries

Hold them to the light

          We had other childhoods
                    where prisms, pattern, anything etched into glass
quickened our imagination

          We have childhoods in us still
                    where the bowl of glass
                              is no trap
                    but molten, glowing, a river

Wood

I.

There are bowls that break.

Not always the most fragile.
Not every poem is gentle.
Some hold old bitterness and won't let go, a root
wrapping around a stone which changes its progress

The grain of wood splits
and we are never prepared for it

Old stories.   Do I hold them or spill them out?
I argue with myself.   There is no need.
No need to say where we've been, to give
the hard history along with the fancy flights of atoms?

Eight years ago we were lovers   I lived in oregon
you came to visit
the dunes, the beach, it was
cranberry festival   you stole me an opal ring
we were thieves then but
you bought yourself
a wooden bowl
myrtlewood   you loved it   I remember

I remember what did not happen to me
as if you transmitted it
        the worry in you lying in sheets across my spirit

        You say this is not my business

Eight years you've said it's not my business

        how your lover smashed the wooden bowl in your kitchen
        how it flew across the room and broke

This simple thing you had for yourself

This simple thing made from wood
its own elemental property
living substance made to hold
our meals, our greens

This simple thing you shared with me
meant to be sturdy, functional,
powerful and ordinary
                              Split
& lost in the violent gesture

                              can't fuse wood back together
        We have to start again
                    from seed

II.

Okay that's my version
and you're still telling me
it's not my business

so much of it had nothing to do with me
so much of it changed my life with you

        I was there   there with you
        and I am here
        throughout it   I watched everything change
and change again
                    I found an end of violence and saw new hope
                    molded carefully, patiently on your lathe
                    the wood not yet able
                    to take the shape   you want

        I know we have to find ways to live
        with what's broken inside us
        and I record what we can't talk about

Aren't you noble?
                    you sneer at me
        caught in this narrow circumference

You want to tell me everything
                    & hate it when I reflect it back to you

The root curving comes to contain
what falls into its grasp
a lens is a bowl
I collect there   a mirror of rain
shaded by my own elements
still when you look
                    there's your face

III.

        It is possible
                            to remake flesh and bone
                            without science, by faith

            but difficult

            We are difficult womyn
            so it must be our fate
            to do difficult things

        Plant new forests   learn the patience
        of creating what we need

        and the strength of trees which widen in wet years
        hold in drought
        each to make her own grain

        even as their roots cleave & collide

We will have new lumber yet
New bowls

            and our same lives
            going forward with both
            what's broken and what's whole

Pottery

A womon can shape a bowl
out of the scattered elements of her feeling
She can invent herself
even now
after the first excitement has gone,
the revolution unwrapped, revealing
broken pots and shards
We have taken years
gluing pieces together   now
we want to start
with new direction

We have the elements inside us
a little copper, a little iron, a little hydrogen,
phosphorus, salt
we can build a kiln between our ribs
the place where the ribs spread apart
is a good place to start construction
brick upon brick of feeling

It's like that with reinventing yourself
you have to go back to the beginning
you have to mix mortar   mud   straw
you have to make the goddam bricks
you have to imagine heat so fierce it could
rearrange the shape of your pottery
you have to go down to the river banks to
get the mud
you have to find the river that someone
sang to you in a song when you were twelve
and you barely remember the words
you have to tie leaves together
to carry the mud back to your town
you have to let the wet clay
dry out the skin of your palms
while you lay your hands
around the waist of your bowl

you have to remember
to light the kiln days before
you can put your bowl in
you have to find the phosphorus lying around
in your armpits   the dry twigs hanging out in your guts
somehow you know how to train the sun on these things
they spark   your kiln glows shudders
will it hold   will it heat
you put your bowl in
too nervous to sleep
the first bowl breaks when you open the door and the cold air
touches it   it was glowing red and now it's fragments
you have to start over
you can start over
you can do what you want to do
you just have to keep doing it
this time   you let the fire die out   the kiln cool
when you open the door
your bowl
shines at you

blue and opalescent

Metal

I hold the metal bowl over a candle flame
heat infuses the base, the rim
I cup the bowl over my face
close my eyes   and breathe

My breath fogs the shine
and I'm pleased for no reason
with the momentary print of my existence
in what will outlast me

Eight metals make a singing bowl.
There are forges in tibet and nepal
where secret elements are mixed
through huge heat   transformed
to bring in sound   through touch.

No ornament
but bowls aren't ornaments —
two sides to each of them.

We focus on what they contain
how sound or light collects
will it keep our food, our treasures, our secrets
safe   we forget
how we hold the bowl ourselves
how the outside
is a drum, or armor, or a breast
how comfortable our hands feel
stroking the contour
our fingers loose
wandering across a rounded plane

Chambers of perception
sounding experience —
we must learn
the art of holding

to make our bowls sing

Night & Sky

I.

Are we held in
or dropped to this place
cupped
or thru the fingers of a careless hand
let loose
to pace and blow across the planet?

Is there a way
to fall outside the sky?

Here is the bowl
that holds you
the bowl so full
so hollow
you cannot touch its shape
nor find escape
from all these other noisy grains
which rub against you
complain & chafe

Here: the night is thick
and full of us

We love our outline in the air
and are created
by the boundaries we create

II.

Our pattern is a thick
condensation of atoms
They say the universe
is different than the earth
this planet an unrepresentative sample
but we knew that, didn't we?

Outside our petty gravity
space and stars are made
of the simplest elements
what's basic, light, naive

They know this because
whatever burns shows its spectral core
what stars consume for fuel
is the clue

How did we ever get so dense?
Imagine us let loose
as hydrogen vapors streaming
the wide cool length
between stars
                        stripped
of props
                no more calcium
copper, lead, uranium

        becoming the
bright primordial building blocks

        a new generation